OWL KNOW HOW

by
Cat Rabbit &
Isobel Knowles

GIBBS SMITH
TO ENRICH AND INSPIRE HUMANKIND

Welcome to Cloud Town.

This is Cornelia Rabbit.
Her best friend, Orvi,
lives next door.

Cornelia likes owls. She likes them better than anything.

She even makes owls.
Cornelia's little owls
can fly around on
their own!

One morning a loud cracking
woke Cornelia from her dreams.

'Look! A horrible branch
monster!' cried Orvi
through the window.

Something very strange
was happening.

Rabbits all over town had the same problem.

Big spiky branches were popping up everywhere.

'It's not a monster. Our cloud is sinking into the treetops!' said Cornelia.

'Do something, quick!' shouted all the rabbits.

Suddenly Cornelia had an idea.
'Owls!' she said.
'We'll need lots of owls.'

Orvi and the others watched as she drew up her plans.

'We must build a factory – an owl factory,' said Cornelia.

All the rabbits worked together
to build the factory. Even
the little rabbits helped.

Alice hammered.

Arlo sawed.

Leo drilled.

Clementine glued.

And Orvi made lunch.

Juniper and Harriet made a big net
and tied it high above the factory.

Cornelia blew
her whistle.

The Owl Factory
sprang into action.

Alice pulled levers.

Arlo turned cogs.

Leo pushed buttons.

Clementine studied screens.

Cornelia made sure each owl was perfect.

And Orvi cheered them all along.

Owls were popping out thick and fast.

It looked like Cornelia's plan was going to work!

'Owls ready?
Owls steady?
Owls GO!'
cried Cornelia.

The owls flapped hard.
Soon the cloud began to rise.

The sharp branches slid away.
The cloud was soft and fluffy again.

'Three cheers for Cornelia
and her Owl Know How!'
shouted Orvi.

Everyone was happy
to be out of the treetops.
Cloud Town was safe
once more.

Cornelia, Orvi and the owls
ate cake to celebrate.

Well done owls.

Well done Cornelia!

The End

A note about the illustrations: Isobel took the photos, Cat made the characters. Together they wrote a story and constructed everything you see in these pages out of felt, cardboard and various other recycled materials.

Manufactured in China in January 2013 by
Imago Australia Pty Ltd

First Edition
17 16 15 14 13   5 4 3 2 1

Originally published by Thames & Hudson Australia Pty Ltd 2012
11 Central Boulevard Portside Business Park
Port Melbourne Victoria 3207

First published in North America by
Gibbs Smith
P.O. Box 667
Layton, Utah 84041

1.800.835.4993 orders
www.gibbs-smith.com

Designed by Tin & Ed
Printed and bound in Singapore

Library of Congress Cataloging-in-Publication Data

Rabbit, Cat.
Owl know how / by Cat Rabbit & Isobel Knowles.
p. cm.
Summary: When Cloud Town begins sinking into the trees, Cornelia Rabbit summons the other rabbits to build owls that can lift the town back into the sky.
ISBN 978-1-4236-3318-1
[1. Clouds‹Fiction. 2. Rabbits‹Fiction. 3. Owls‹Fiction.] I. Knowles, Isobel. II. Title.
PZ7.R1038Owl 2013
[E]‹dc23
2012037726